READING LOG

&

BOOK JOURNAL

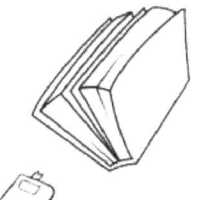

by Maryn Patrice Sherton

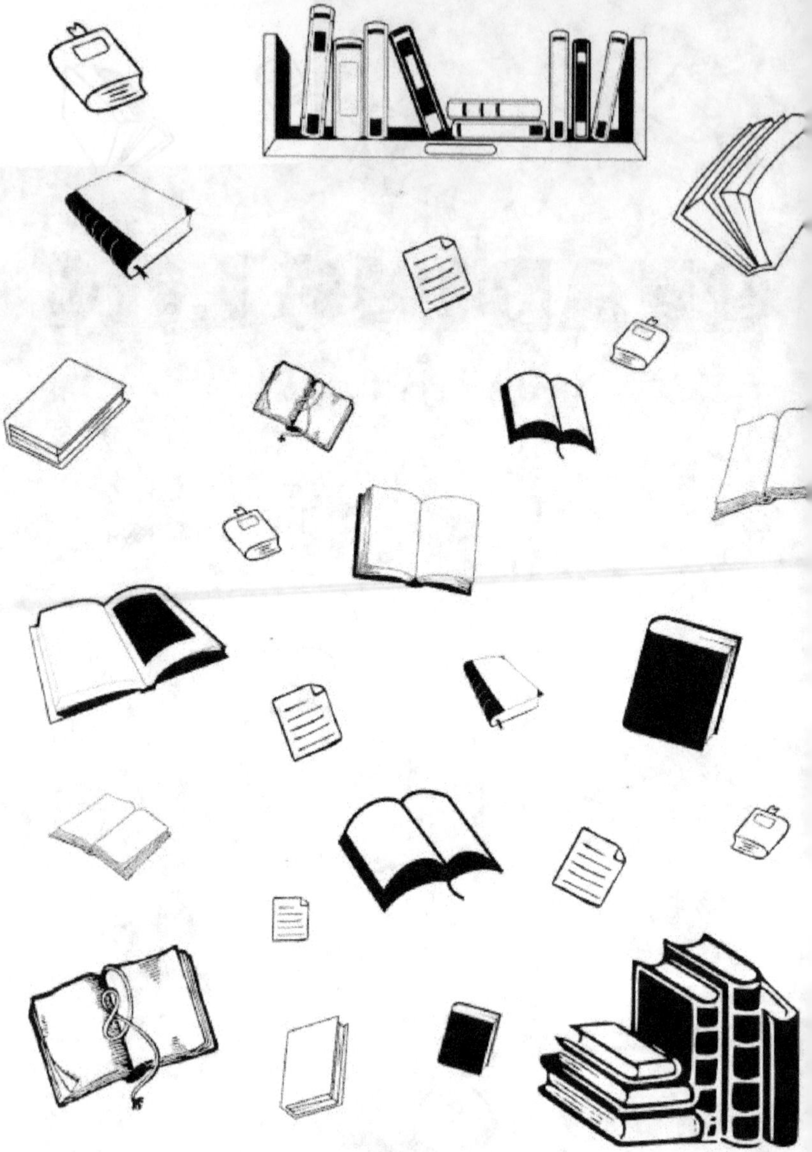

KI PRODUCTIONS

Where every story matters

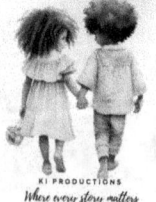

This journal belongs to:

Reading Log

TITLE		DATE	PAG
AUTHOR			
		DATE	PAG
		DATE	PAG
		DATE	PAG
		DATE	PAG
		DATE	PAGE

Completion Date:

Book Selection

Book title	*Author*	*Genre*

Plot

Setting/Time

Characters

Themes & Motifs

Discussion Questions or Topics:

Book Review & Reflection

TITLE

AUTHOR

GENRE

DUCKS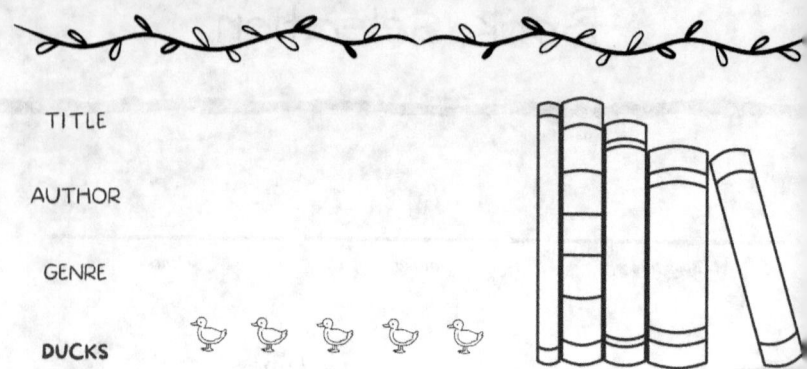

QUESTIONS

FAVORITE MOMENT OR CHAPTER

Other Thoughts

ok Summary

TITLE	
AUTHOR	
SETTING	
PROTAGONIST	

SUMMARY

Favorite Quotes

BY	
QUOTE	
BY	
QUOTE	
BY	
QUOTE	
BY	
QUOTE	
BY	
QUOTE	

to do List

- ☐ ....
- ☐ ....
- ☐ ....
- ☐ ....
- ☐ ....
- ☐ ....
- ☐ ....
- ☐ ....
- ☐ ....
- ☐ ....

_____

_____

_____

_____

_____

_____

_____

_____

_____

_____

_____

_____

_____

_____

_____

_____

_____

_____

_____

_____

_____

_____

_____

_____

_____

_____

TLE

THOR

	DATE	PAGES

	DATE	PAGES

	DATE	PAGES

	DATE	PAGES

	DATE	PAGES

	DATE	PAGES

pletion Date:

Book Selection

_____   _____   _____
   Book title   _Author_   _Genre_

Plot   Setting/Time

Characters   Themes & Motifs

Discussion Questions or Topics:

ok Review & Reflection

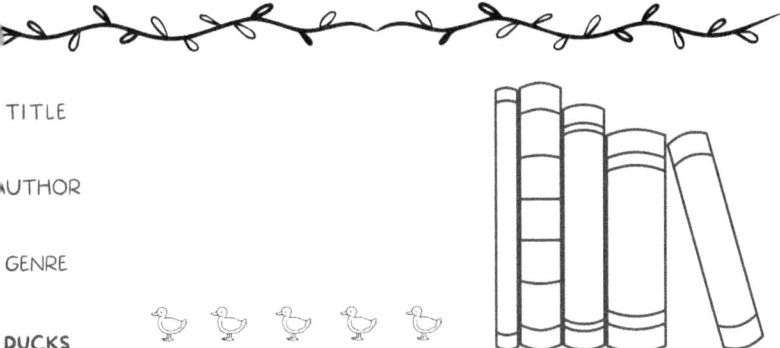

TITLE

UTHOR

GENRE

DUCKS

QUESTIONS

FAVORITE MOMENT OR CHAPTER

er Thoughts

Book Summary

TITLE	
AUTHOR	
SETTING	
PROTAGONIST	

SUMMARY

vorite Quotes

BY	
QUOTE	
BY	
QUOTE	
BY	
QUOTE	
BY	
QUOTE	
BY	
QUOTE	

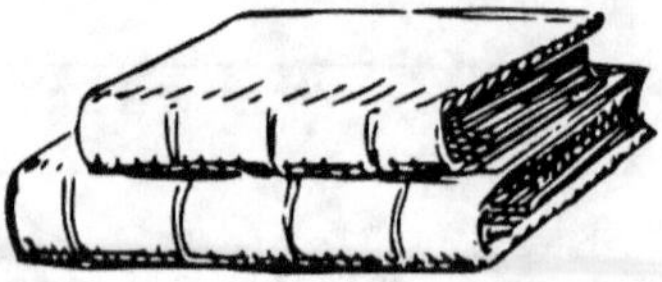

_____

_____

_____

_____

_____

_____

_____

_____

_____

_____

_____

_____

_____

to do List

- [ ] ....
- [ ] ....
- [ ] ....
- [ ] ....
- [ ] ....
- [ ] ....
- [ ] ....
- [ ] ....
- [ ] ....
- [ ] ....

_____

_____

_____

_____

_____

_____

_____

_____

_____

_____

_____

_____

_____

_____

_____

_____

_____

_____

_____

_____

_____

_____

_____

_____

_____

_____

_____

_____

_____

_____

_____

_____

_____

_____

_____

_____

_____

_____

_____

_____

_____

_____

_____

_____

_____

_____

Reading Log

TITLE		DATE	PAG
AUTHOR			
		DATE	PAG
		DATE	PAG
		DATE	PAG
		DATE	PAG
		DATE	PAG

Completion Date:

Book Selection

_____   _____   _____
Book title   *Author*   *Genre*

Plot   Setting/Time

_____   _____
_____   _____
_____   _____
_____   _____

Characters   Themes & Motifs

_____   _____
_____   _____
_____   _____

Discussion Questions or Topics:

Book Review & Reflection

TITLE

AUTHOR

GENRE

DUCKS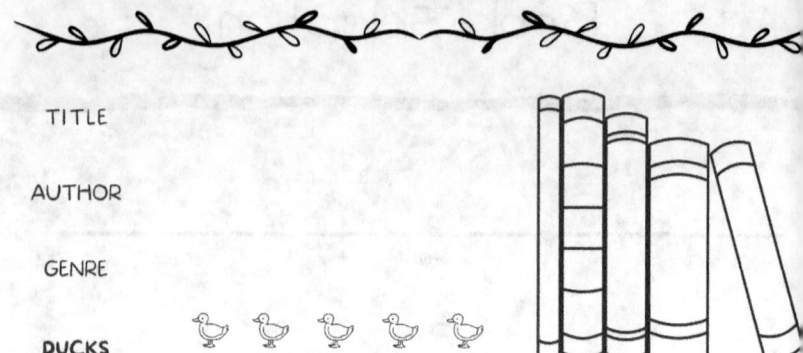

QUESTIONS

FAVORITE MOMENT OR CHAPTER

Other Thoughts

TITLE	
AUTHOR	
SETTING	
PROTAGONIST	

SUMMARY

Favorite Quotes

BY	
QUOTE	

BY	
QUOTE	

BY	
QUOTE	

BY	
QUOTE	

BY	
QUOTE	

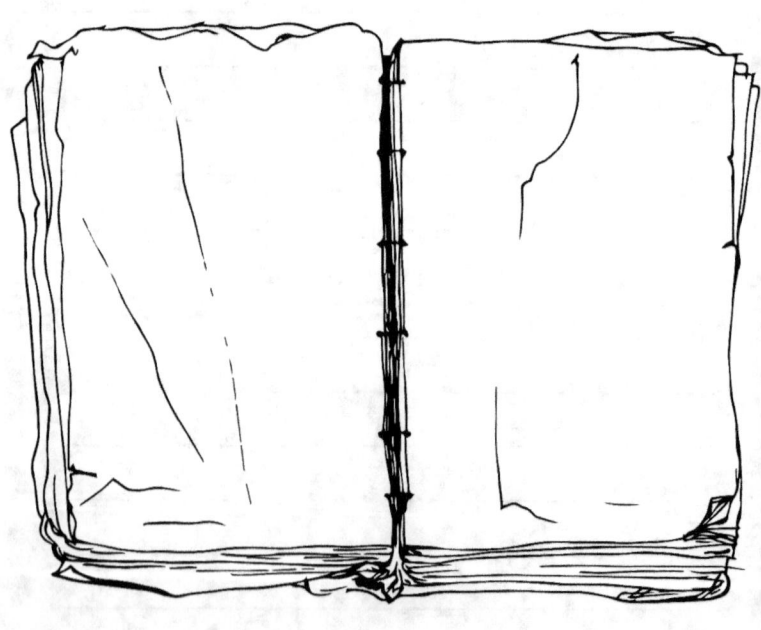

to do List

- ☐ ....
- ☐ ....
- ☐ ....
- ☐ ....
- ☐ ....
- ☐ ....
- ☐ ....
- ☐ ....
- ☐ ....
- ☐ ....

_____
_____
_____
_____
_____
_____
_____
_____
_____
_____
_____
_____

_____
_____
_____
_____
_____
_____
_____
_____
_____
_____
_____
_____
_____

TLE

THOR

	DATE	PAGES

	DATE	PAGES

	DATE	PAGES

	DATE	PAGES

	DATE	PAGES

	DATE	PAGES

pletion Date:

Book Selection

_____   _____   _____
        Book title   Author   Genre

Plot   Setting/Time
_____   _____
_____   _____
_____   _____
_____   _____
_____   _____

Characters   Themes & Motifs
_____   _____
_____   _____
_____   _____
_____   _____

Discussion Questions or Topics:

ok Review & Reflection

TITLE

UTHOR

GENRE

DUCKS

QUESTIONS

FAVORITE MOMENT OR CHAPTER

er Thoughts

Books Summary

TITLE	
AUTHOR	
SETTING	
PROTAGONIST	

SUMMARY

BY

QUOTE

BY

QUOTE

BY

QUOTE

BY

QUOTE

BY

QUOTE

_____

_____

_____

_____

_____

_____

_____

_____

_____

_____

_____

_____

_____

_____

_____

_____

_____

_____

_____

_____

_____

_____

_____

_____

_____

_____

to do List

- ☐ ....
- ☐ ....
- ☐ ....
- ☐ ....
- ☐ ....
- ☐ ....
- ☐ ....
- ☐ ....
- ☐ ....
- ☐ ....

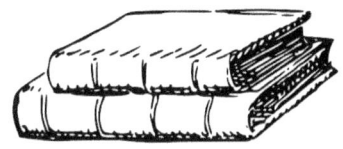

Reading Log

TITLE		DATE	PAG
AUTHOR			
		DATE	PAG
		DATE	PAG
		DATE	PAG
		DATE	PAG
		DATE	PAG

Completion Date:

Book Selection

Book title	*Author*	*Genre*

Plot

Setting/Time

Characters

Themes & Motifs

Discussion Questions or Topics:

Book Review & Reflection

TITLE

AUTHOR

GENRE

DUCKS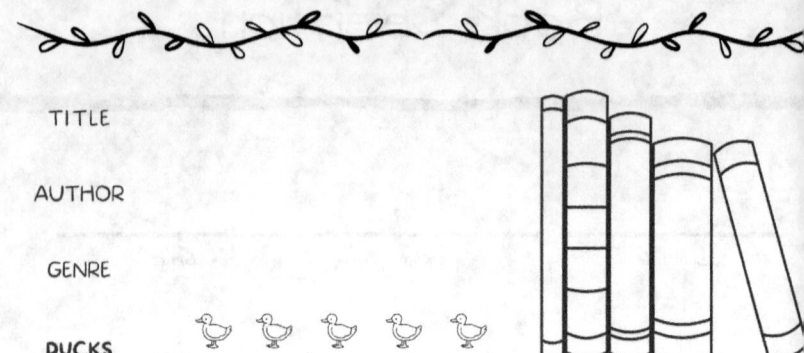

QUESTIONS

FAVORITE MOMENT OR CHAPTER

Other Thoughts

oks Summary

TITLE	
AUTHOR	
SETTING	
PROTAGONIST	

SUMMARY

Favorite Quotes

BY	
QUOTE	
BY	
QUOTE	
BY	
QUOTE	
BY	
QUOTE	
BY	
QUOTE	

_____

_____

_____

_____

_____

_____

_____

_____

_____

_____

_____

_____

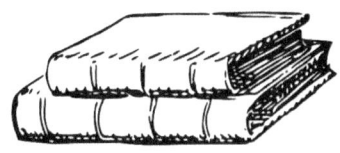

_____

_____

_____

_____

_____

_____

_____

_____

_____

_____

_____

_____

_____

to do List

- ☐ ....
- ☐ ....
- ☐ ....
- ☐ ....
- ☐ ....
- ☐ ....
- ☐ ....
- ☐ ....
- ☐ ....
- ☐ ....

_____

_____

_____

_____

_____

_____

_____

_____

_____

_____

_____

_____

_____

_____

_____

_____

_____

_____

_____

_____

_____

_____

_____

_____

ading Log

TLE		DATE	PAGES
THOR			
		DATE	PAGES
		DATE	PAGES
		DATE	PAGES
		DATE	PAGES
		DATE	PAGES

pletion Date:

Book Selection

Book title	Author	Genre

Plot

Setting/Time

Characters

Themes & Motifs

Discussion Questions or Topics:

ok Review & Reflection

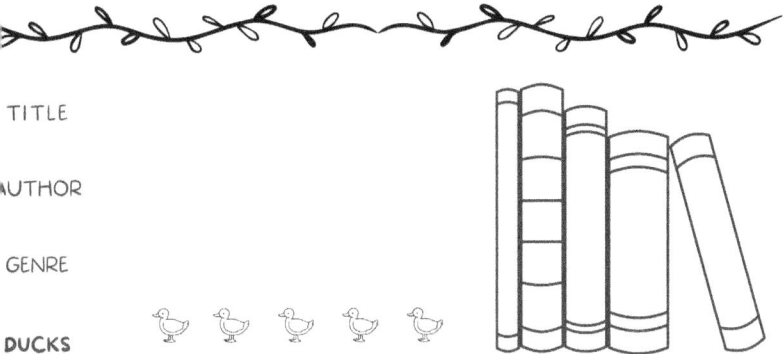

TITLE

UTHOR

GENRE

DUCKS

QUESTIONS

FAVORITE MOMENT OR CHAPTER

er Thoughts

Books Summary

TITLE	
AUTHOR	
SETTING	
PROTAGONIST	

SUMMARY

BY

QUOTE

BY

QUOTE

BY

QUOTE

BY

QUOTE

BY

QUOTE

_____

_____

_____

_____

_____

_____

_____

_____

_____

_____

_____

_____

to do List

- [ ] ....
- [ ] ....
- [ ] ....
- [ ] ....
- [ ] ....
- [ ] ....
- [ ] ....
- [ ] ....
- [ ] ....
- [ ] ....

_____

_____

_____

_____

_____

_____

_____

_____

_____

_____

_____

_____

_____

_____

_____

_____

_____

_____

_____

_____

_____

_____

_____

_____

_____

_____

_____

_____

_____

_____

_____

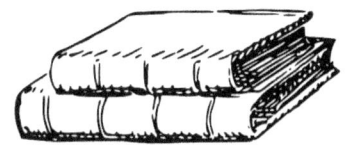

Reading Log

TITLE		DATE	PAG
AUTHOR			
		DATE	PAG
		DATE	PAG
		DATE	PAG
		DATE	PAG
		DATE	PAG

Completion Date:

Book Selection

| Book title | Author | Genre |

Plot

Setting/Time

Characters

Themes & Motifs

Discussion Questions or Topics:

Book Review & Reflection

TITLE

AUTHOR

GENRE

DUCKS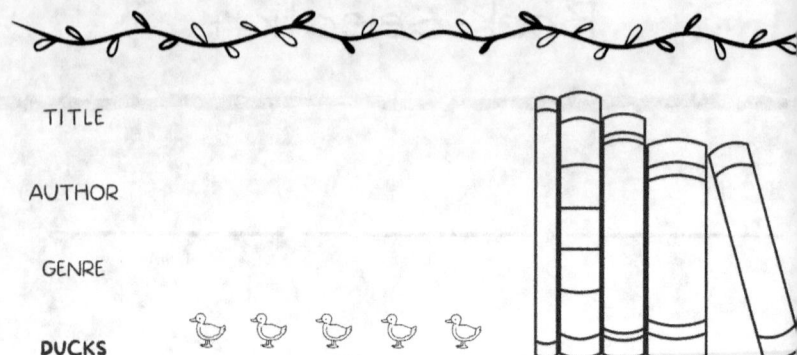

QUESTIONS

FAVORITE MOMENT OR CHAPTER

Other Thoughts

TITLE	
AUTHOR	
SETTING	
PROTAGONIST	

SUMMARY

Favorite Quotes

BY	
QUOTE	

BY	
QUOTE	

BY	
QUOTE	

BY	
QUOTE	

BY	
QUOTE	

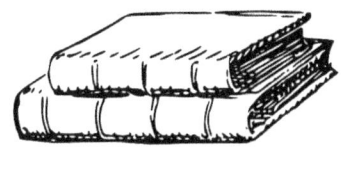

_____

_____

_____

_____

_____

_____

_____

_____

_____

_____

_____

_____

_____

to do List

- ☐ ....
- ☐ ....
- ☐ ....
- ☐ ....
- ☐ ....
- ☐ ....
- ☐ ....
- ☐ ....
- ☐ ....
- ☐ ....

ading Log

TLE

THOR

	DATE	PAGES
	DATE	PAGES
	DATE	PAGES
	DATE	PAGES
	DATE	PAGES
	DATE	PAGES

pletion Date:

Book Selection

_____ _____ _____
Book title   *Author*   *Genre*

Plot   Setting/Time
_____   _____
_____   _____
_____   _____
_____   _____
_____   _____

Characters   Themes & Motifs
_____   _____
_____   _____
_____   _____
_____   _____
_____   _____

Discussion Questions or Topics:

ok Review & Reflection

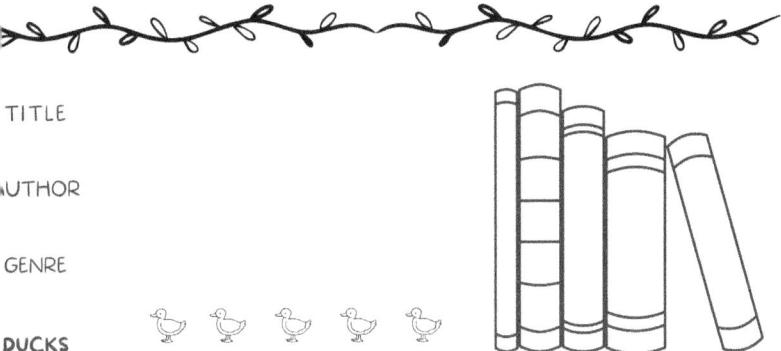

TITLE

UTHOR

GENRE

DUCKS

QUESTIONS

FAVORITE MOMENT OR CHAPTER

er Thoughts

Books Summary

TITLE	
AUTHOR	
SETTING	
PROTAGONIST	

SUMMARY

Favorite Quotes

BY

QUOTE

BY

QUOTE

BY

QUOTE

BY

QUOTE

BY

QUOTE

to do List

- [ ] ....
- [ ] ....
- [ ] ....
- [ ] ....
- [ ] ....
- [ ] ....
- [ ] ....
- [ ] ....
- [ ] ....
- [ ] ....

_____

_____

_____

_____

_____

_____

_____

_____

_____

_____

_____

_____

_____

TLE		DATE	PAGES
HOR			
		DATE	PAGES
		DATE	PAGES
		DATE	PAGES
		DATE	PAGES
		DATE	PAGES

pletion Date:

Book Selection

_____   _____   _____
Book title   *Author*   *Genre*

Plot
_____
_____
_____
_____
_____

Setting/Time
_____
_____
_____
_____
_____

Characters
_____
_____
_____
_____

Themes & Motifs
_____
_____
_____
_____

Discussion Questions or Topics:

ok Review & Reflection

TITLE

UTHOR

GENRE

DUCKS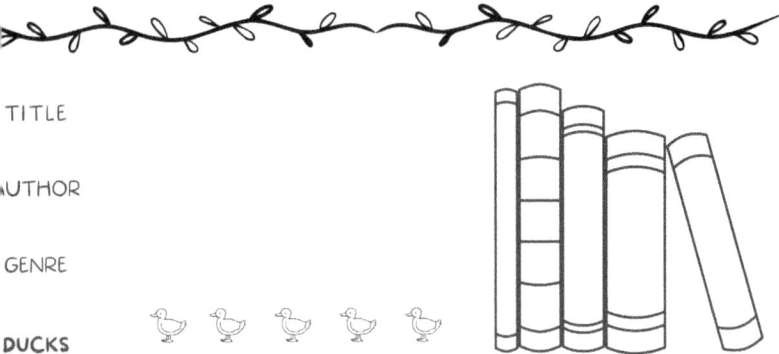

QUESTIONS

FAVORITE MOMENT OR CHAPTER

er Thoughts

Books Summary

TITLE	
AUTHOR	
SETTING	
PROTAGONIST	

SUMMARY

BY

QUOTE

BY

QUOTE

BY

QUOTE

BY

QUOTE

BY

QUOTE

to do List

- [ ] ....
- [ ] ....
- [ ] ....
- [ ] ....
- [ ] ....
- [ ] ....
- [ ] ....
- [ ] ....
- [ ] ....
- [ ] ....

_____

_____

_____

_____

_____

_____

_____

_____

_____

_____

_____

_____

_____

_____

_____

_____

_____

_____

_____

_____

_____

_____

_____

_____

TLE   DATE   PAGES

THOR

                                             DATE   PAGES

                                             DATE   PAGES

                                             DATE   PAGES

                                             DATE   PAGES

                                             DATE   PAGES

mpletion Date:

Book Selection

_____   _____   _____
Book title   *Author*   *Genre*

Plot

_____
_____
_____
_____
_____

Setting/Time

_____
_____
_____
_____

Characters

_____
_____
_____
_____

Themes & Motifs

_____
_____
_____
_____

Discussion Questions or Topics:

ok Review & Reflection

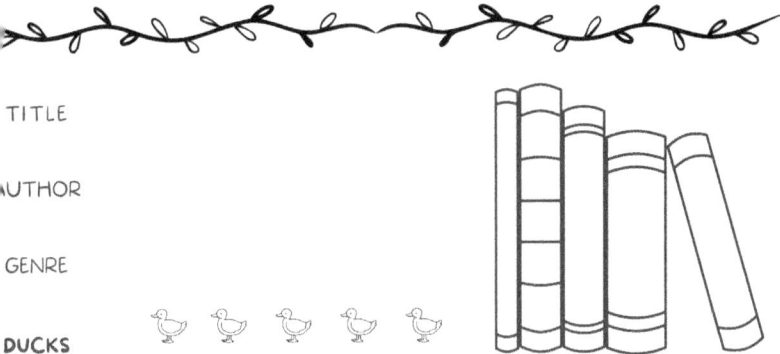

TITLE

UTHOR

GENRE

DUCKS

QUESTIONS

FAVORITE MOMENT OR CHAPTER

er Thoughts

Book Summary

TITLE	
AUTHOR	
SETTING	
PROTAGONIST	

SUMMARY

vorite Quotes

BY

QUOTE

BY

QUOTE

BY

QUOTE

BY

QUOTE

BY

QUOTE

_____

_____

_____

_____

_____

_____

_____

_____

_____

_____

_____

_____

_____

_____

_____

_____

_____

_____

_____

_____

to do List

- [ ] ....
- [ ] ....
- [ ] ....
- [ ] ....
- [ ] ....
- [ ] ....
- [ ] ....
- [ ] ....
- [ ] ....
- [ ] ....

_____

_____

_____

_____

_____

_____

_____

_____

_____

_____

_____

_____

_____

READ
READ
READ

www.ingramcontent.com/pod-product-compliance
Lightning Source LLC
Chambersburg PA
CBHW071005120626
46546CB00003B/937